ATLANTIS

BY LISA OWINGS

EPIC

BELLWETHER MEDIA • MINNEAPOLIS, MN

EPIC BOOKS are no ordinary books. They burst with intense action, high-speed heroics, and shadows of the unknown. Are you ready for an Epic adventure?

This edition first published in 2015 by Bellwether Media, Inc.

No part of this publication may be reproduced in whole or in part without written permission of the publisher. For information regarding permission, write to Bellwether Media, Inc., Attention: Permissions Department, 5357 Penn Avenue South, Minneapolis, MN 55419.

Library of Congress Cataloging-in-Publication Data

Owings, Lisa.
   Atlantis / by Lisa Owings.
      pages cm. – (Epic: Unexplained Mysteries)
   Includes bibliographical references and index.
   Summary: "Engaging images accompany information about Atlantis. The combination of high-interest subject matter and light text is intended for students in grades 2 through 7"– Provided by publisher.
   Audience: Ages 7-12.
   ISBN 978-1-62617-200-5 (hardcover : alk. paper)
   1. Atlantis (Legendary place)–Juvenile literature. I. Title.
   GN751.O88 2015
   398.23′4–dc23
                              2014034954

Designed by Jon Eppard.

Printed in the United States of America, North Mankato, MN.

TABLE OF CONTENTS

MYSTERY AT SEA

A diver slips into the sea. She swims among the bright fish and corals. Suddenly the current sweeps her onto the reef. She gasps as rough coral scrapes against her.

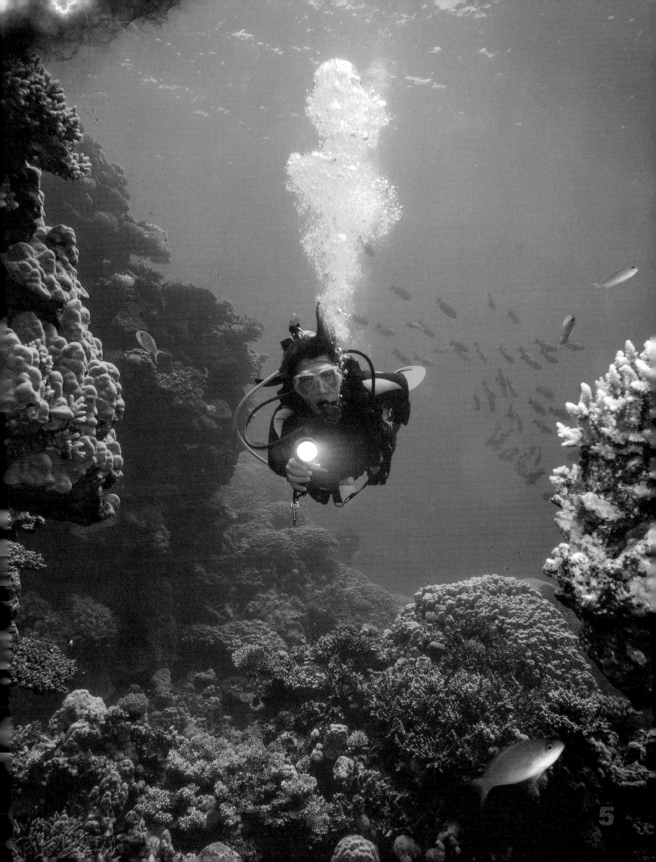

Then she sees it is not coral at all. She has crashed into an old, broken statue. Nearby are other bits of stone. Her eyes widen in surprise. Could she have found the ruins of Atlantis?

PLATO'S ATLANTIS

Atlantis was first described about 2,400 years ago. The Greek thinker Plato wrote of a beautiful island in the Atlantic Ocean. A great city stood at its center.

Plato

Poseidon

THE RINGED CITY

The Greek sea god Poseidon watched over Atlantis. He carved three rings of water around the city to protect it.

Italy

Egypt

A LOST EMPIRE

The kingdom of Atlantis ruled over many surrounding lands. Its power stretched to Egypt and Italy.

N
W · E
S

The people of Atlantis were powerful. At first they were strong, wise, and kind. But they became wicked over time. The gods decided to punish them.

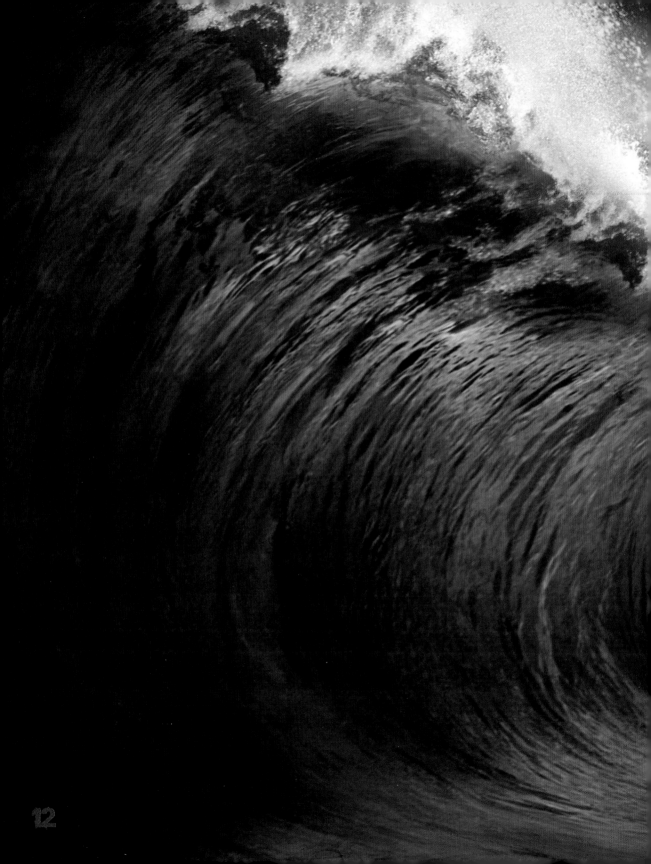

Earthquakes tore at
the island. Mighty waves
crashed over the city.
In one day, Atlantis sank
forever beneath the sea.

13

LOST OR IMAGINED?

The legend of Atlantis has been debated since Plato's time. Skeptics think Plato made it up to teach a lesson. They argue there is no proof Atlantis existed. A sunken island would be hard to miss.

Other people believe Atlantis was real. Large volcanoes have caused similar disasters. Many people think the legend was about an eruption in the Greek islands.

Greece

Santorini →

Crete

A TRUE STORY?

A volcano on the Greek island Santorini erupted around 1500 BCE. The blast destroyed a society on the nearby island of Crete.

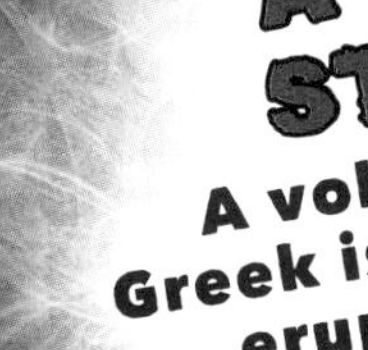

N
W ✦ E
S

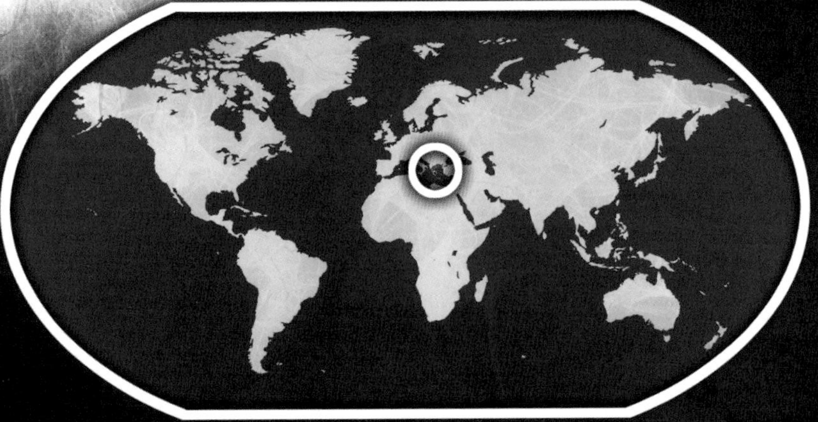

Some believers search for Atlantis. They use sonar and other technology. People have claimed to find Atlantis in many places.

POSSIBLE LOCATIONS OF ATLANTIS

People have found ruins all over the world that match Plato's descriptions of Atlantis.

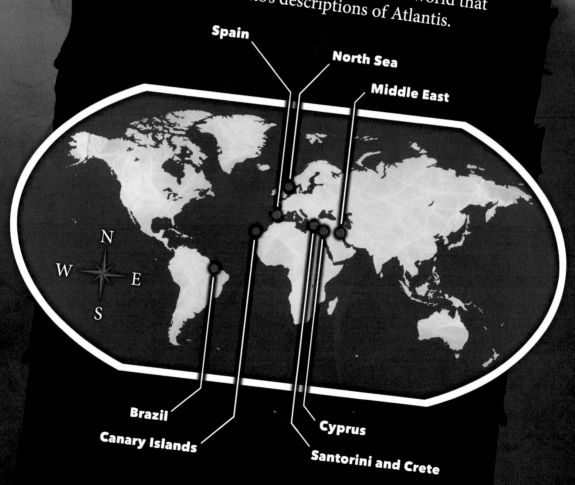

Spain

North Sea

Middle East

N
W — E
S

Brazil

Canary Islands

Cyprus

Santorini and Crete

Is Atlantis still waiting to be found? Or was it all in Plato's mind? We may never know. And we may never stop searching for this lost world.

GLOSSARY

corals—small ocean animals whose skeletons make up reefs

debated—thought or talked about something from different points of view

earthquakes—disasters in which the ground shakes from the movement of Earth's crust

eruption—when hot, melted rock called lava shoots out of a volcano

legend—a story many people believe that has not been proven true

reef—a structure made of coral that usually forms in shallow seawater

ruins—the physical remains of a human-made structure

skeptics—people who doubt the truth of something

sonar—a system of finding objects in the water

volcanoes—holes in the earth where melted rock comes through

TO LEARN MORE

At the Library

Hawkins, John. *Atlantis and Other Lost Worlds*. New York, N.Y.: PowerKids Press, 2012.

Matthews, Rupert. *Ancient Mysteries*. Mankato, Minn.: QEB Pub., 2010.

McClellan, Ray. *The Loch Ness Monster*. Minneapolis, Minn.: Bellwether Media, 2014.

On the Web

Learning more about Atlantis is as easy as 1, 2, 3.

1. Go to www.factsurfer.com.

2. Enter "Atlantis" into the search box.

3. Click the "Surf" button and you will see a list of related web sites.

With factsurfer.com, finding more information is just a click away.

INDEX

The images in this book are reproduced through the courtesy of: Jon Eppard, front cover, pp. 6-7, 10, 11, 17, 19; timsimages, pp. 4-5; Pascal Deloche/ Godong/ Corbis, p. 8; G.K., p. 9 (top); Racheal Grazias, p. 9 (bottom); Mel-nik, pp. 12-13; Anastasios71, p. 14; Linda Bucklin, p. 15; Nigge/ Mauritius/ SuperStock, p. 16; 71989651, p. 18; Digital Storm, pp. 20-21.